GW00758535

THIS BOOK BELONGS TO...

Name: Age:

Favourite player:

2023/24

	My Predictions	Actual
The Sky Blues' final position:		
The Sky Blues' top scorer:		
Championship winners:		
Championship top scorer:		
FA Cup winners:		
EFL Cup winners:		

Contributors: Peter Rogers

A TWOCAN PUBLICATION

©2023. Published by twocan under licence from Coventry City Football Club.

Every effort has been made to ensure the accuracy of information within this publication but the publishers cannot be held responsible for any errors or omissions. Views expressed are those of the authors and do not necessarily represent those of the publishers or the football club. All rights reserved.

978-1-915571-56-4

£10

CONTENTS

Simon
MOORE

1

POSITION: Goalkeeper   **COUNTRY: England**   **DOB: 19/05/1990**

Simon Moore joined the Sky Blues in July 2021 on a three-year contract. Moore established himself as a prominent member of the starting eleven in his first season with the Sky Blues, appearing in 42 games across all competitions and keeping nine clean sheets.

Luis
BINKS

2

POSITION: Defender   **COUNTRY: England**   **DOB: 02/09/2001**

Binks began his career in the Tottenham Hotspur Academy, featuring heavily for their Under 18s and 21s before leaving Spurs in February 2020 to sign a professional contract with Montreal Impact in the MLS.

He would play eight games for Impact before he caught the attention of Bologna, moving to the Italian side in August 2020 - though he would complete the 2020 MLS season at Montreal, playing a further 17 games for them.

Binks made his Bologna debut in September 2021 and has made 15 appearances so far in Serie A for the Club. The 22/23 season would see Luis enjoy a 34-game loan spell at Serie B side Como.

Jay
DASILVA

3

POSITION: Defender   **COUNTRY:** Jamaica   **DOB:** 22/04/1998

Jay Dasilva joined the Sky Blues in July 2023, making him the first signing of the summer. Jay progressed through the Chelsea youth system, where he won the UEFA Youth League twice and the FA Youth Cup three times. Dasilva later joined Bristol City initially on loan for the 2018/19 season and has since made 144 appearances while scoring twice.

Bobby
THOMAS

4

POSITION: Defender   **COUNTRY:** England   **DOB:** 30/01/02

Following the agreement of an undisclosed fee between the Sky Blues and Burnley, the 22-year-old agreed to a four-year contract with City. Last season saw Thomas have loan spells at two sides in League One. He began the campaign at Bristol Rovers, where he would play 26 games in all competitions and score three goals.

During the January transfer window Thomas joined Barnsley on loan and he would feature prominently as the Tykes reached the League One Play-Off Final, playing 25 games and netting three times.

Kyle McFADZEAN — 5

POSITION: Defender **COUNTRY:** England **DOB:** 20/02/1987

Kyle McFadzean joined the Sky Blues in June 2019 after his contract with Burton Albion expired. The seasoned defender established himself as a defensive leader, helping them to the League One title and a fourth promotion of his career. City's vice-captain continues being a vital cog in Mark Robins' defence.

Liam KELLY — 6

POSITION: Midfielder **COUNTRY:** Scotland **DOB:** 10/02/1990

Club captain Liam Kelly joined the club in 2017 and became a crucial figure in the Sky Blues' return to League One, playing the full 90 minutes in the League Two Play-Off final. Kelly then captained the Sky Blues side to a League One title and earned promotion back to the Championship. Despite being out injured for most of the season Kelly played a crucial role in guiding the team to the Championship Play-Off final last season.

Tatsuhiro
SAKAMOTO 7

POSITION: Midfielder   **COUNTRY:** Japan   **DOB:** 22/10/1996

The Japanese international midfielder joined the Sky Blues from Belgian club KV Oostende in July 2023. Tatsuhiro started his professional football career with the J2 league team Montedio before switching to the J1 league team Cerezo Osaka. Sakamoto earned a move to Belgian side KV Oostende initially on loan, Sakamoto participated in 81 games with Oostende in all, recording ten goals. Tats has also represented Japan on two separate occasions, as well as being part of the World Cup squad in 2022.

Jamie
ALLEN 8

POSITION: Midfielder   **COUNTRY:** England   **DOB:** 29/01/1995

Jamie Allen joined the Sky Blues from Burton Albion in 2019. Allen arrived at the Sky Blues with a vast amount of experience, having made over 230 career appearances, scoring 20 goals. Allen became a key member during the 2019/20 season as the Sky Blues won the League One title. The 2021/22 and 2022/23 seasons saw Jamie enjoy his best run of appearances in the City side.

Ellis
SIMMS

9

POSITION: Forward **COUNTRY:** England **DOB:** 05/01/2001

Ellis joined the Sky Blues in July 2023 from Everton. Ellis joined Everton as a 16-year-old and enjoyed three successful loan spells away from Goodison Park. Last season Sunderland signed Simms and he netted seven goals in 17 games in the Championship before being recalled by Everton in January, where he would feature eleven times and score once in the top-flight - a vital late equaliser against Chelsea.

Callum
O'HARE
10

POSITION: Midfielder   **COUNTRY: England**   **DOB: 01/05/1998**

After joining Sky Blues initially on loan, Callum O'Hare joined permanently in 2020. Callum had an instant effect during his first year with the team and was crucial in helping the Sky Blues win the League One title. O'Hare returned to the Sky Blues permanently for the 2020/21 season and became the only player to participate in every league game. O'Hare's performances were recognised by the supporters and players as he was named the Players' Player, Young Player and Player of the Season, he was also name JSB Player of the Year in 2021/22.

Haji
WRIGHT
11

POSITION: Forward   **COUNTRY: USA**   **DOB: 27/03/1998**

The USA international striker completed a move from Antalyaspor following the agreement of a club-record transfer fee. Wright began his career at New York Cosmos, joining Schalke 04 in Germany in 2016. Following his spell there, which also included a loan with SV Sandhausen, Wright joined Dutch side VVV-Venlo for the 2019/20 campaign. In 2020 Haji made the move to Danish Superliga club SønderjyskE, where he scored 13 goals in 37 games.

The 2021/22 season saw Wright move to Antalyaspor on loan and he scored 15 goals in 35 games during his temporary spell, including a hat-trick on his debut. The transfer was made permanent in July 2022 and Wright would net a further 16 goals in 29 games for the Turkish Superlig side.

Haji has represented the USA seven times at senior level, scoring two goals and representing his country at the 2022 World Cup, playing all four matches including starting against England.

Ben
WILSON

13

POSITION: Goalkeeper   **COUNTRY:** England   **DOB:** 09/08/1992

Wilson joined the Sky Blues after leaving Bradford City in 2019. The 2022/23 season was a breakthrough season for Ben as he broke the Club record for most clean sheets in a season along with winning the Championship Golden Glove. Wilson also scored a last-minute equaliser against Blackburn Rovers to earn a massive point towards the Sky Blues' Play-Off push.

Ben
SHEAF

14

POSITION: **Midfielder**   COUNTRY: **England**   DOB: **05/02/1998**

Ben Sheaf joined the Sky Blues on loan from Arsenal for the 2020/21 season before making the transfer permanent the following season. The midfielder became a key man in the middle, making over 30 appearances in each of his two campaigns. Sheaf played a vital role in the Sky Blues side which went on to narrowly missing out on promotion to the Premier League.

Liam
KITCHING

15

POSITION: **Defender**   COUNTRY: **England**   DOB: **25/09/1999**

Harrogate-born Kitching began his career at Leeds United, joining his hometown side on loan in January 2018 and netting three goals in ten games in National League North.

Having impressed at Town, Forest Green Rovers swooped in for Kitching at the start of the 2019/20 season for an undisclosed fee. Liam would make 53 appearances for the Gloucestershire side in his eighteen months at the League Two side.

His form at Rovers caught the attention of Barnsley and Kitching moved to Yorkshire in January 2021. He would go on to play 93 games for the Oakwell club, scoring on six occasions, and would skipper the side as the Club reached the 2023 League One Play-Off final.

Joel
LATIBEAUDIERE
22

POSITION: Defender **COUNTRY:** Jamaica **DOB:** 06/01/2000

Jamaican international Latibeaudiere started his career at Manchester City, captaining City's under-18s to the Premier League North title and also being part of the side that reached the FA Youth Cup final. In October 2020, Latibeaudiere moved to Swansea City. In a three-season spell in South Wales he played a total of 79 games, scoring on three occasions.

Doncaster-born and of Jamaican descent, Joel was a member of the England Under 17 side that finished runners-up in the 2017 UEFA European Championships and then lifted the 2017 Under 17s FIFA World Cup, playing the full game as England beat Spain.

He would play for England up to Under 20 level before going on to represent Jamaica and has currently got six caps, with his most recent appearances coming in the 2023 CONCACAF Gold Cup.

Jake
BIDWELL
21

POSITION: Defender **COUNTRY:** England **DOB:** 21/03/1993

Jake Bidwell signed a three-and-a-half-year contract with the Sky Blues in January 2022 following three years with Swansea City. Jake was a Goalkeeper in his first two seasons while coming through the ranks at Everton, before switching to left-back, working his way up to the club's U18 team. Bidwell played a very important role in 2022/23 season making 49 appearances.

Matty
GODDEN
24

POSITION: Forward **COUNTRY:** England **DOB:** 29/07/1991

Matty Godden joined the Sky Blues in August 2019 from Peterborough. In his maiden season with City, he helped fire the club to the League One title and promotion back to the Championship scoring 16 goals. Godden's goals saw him end the year as the Club's top goalscorer and his performances didn't go unnoticed, as he was named in the PFA League One Team of the Year for the 2019/20 season. Godden continued to show his goal-scoring ability in the Championship, scoring 26 goals in just over 80 appearances.

Yasin
AYARI
26

POSITION: Midfielder **COUNTRY:** Sweden **DOB:** 06/10/2003

Yasin made his professional debut in December 2020 for AIK at the age of just 17, having progressed through the youth ranks. He would go on to make a total of 48 appearances for the Swedish club, netting six goals.

In January 2023 Ayari moved to the English Premier League with Brighton and Hove Albion for an undisclosed fee, signing a four-year contract. He made his Albion debut in March during the 5-0 FA Cup win over Grimsby Town and played three times in the Premier League last season, making his full debut in May.

Yasin represented his native Sweden at Under 17, Under 19 and Under 21 before making his full international debut against Finland, picking up another cap in a friendly with Iceland.

Milan
VAN EWIJK
27

POSITION: Defender   **COUNTRY:** Netherlands   **DOB:** 08/09/2000

The 22-year-old began his career in the Feyenoord academy in his Dutch homeland, before moving to Excelsior Maassluis where he played 36 games and scored 2 goals in the 2018/19 campaign.

Milan's form there captured the eye of then Eredivisie side ADO Den Haag and he would play 46 times for them, scoring one goal. He made the move to SC Heerenveen in 2021 and played 78 games for the Club, scoring seven goals.

Milan's performances have earned him international recognition too, appearing 8 times for the Holland Under 21 side.

Josh
ECCLES

28

POSITION: Midfielder **COUNTRY:** England **DOB:** 06/04/2000

Josh Eccles continued the proud history of the academy promoting youth players into the first team when he signed his first deal with the club. He made his debut for the Sky Blues when he started in midfield at the Jonny Rocks Stadium against Cheltenham Town in EFL Trophy. Eccles was given additional first-team opportunities in the 2019/20 season, including his football league debut and first start in a 2-1 win over Rochdale. Josh made 37 appearances in the 2022/23 season including three in the Play-Offs, he also scored his first goal for the club against Birmingham City back in April.

Fabio
TAVARES

30

POSITION: Forward **COUNTRY:** Portugal **DOB:** 22/01/2001

Fabio Tavares agreed to join the Sky Blues from Rochdale during the January Transfer Window of January 2021. Fabio impressed with the Under-21s and helped his side win the Professional Development League, which earned him seven appearances in the Championship during the season. He scored a last-minute screamer against Preston North End to earn a point back at the start of 2022. Fabio made nine appearances in the 2022/23 season.

Bradley COLLINS 40

POSITION: Goalkeeper   **COUNTRY:** England   **DOB:** 18/02/1997

Southampton-born Collins began his career at Chelsea's Academy where he would win the UEFA Youth League and FA Youth Cup and feature prominently for the Club's Development squad. In 2017/18 he enjoyed a season-long loan at Forest Green Rovers in League Two and played 45 games. The next season saw Collins at Burton Albion on loan in League One, where would make a total of 35 appearances.

Following the expiry of his contract at Chelsea in the summer of 2019, he moved into the Championship with Barnsley. In four seasons with the Tykes, Collins made a total of 117 appearances and won their Player of the Season award in 2021/22.

Marco RUS 43

POSITION: Midfielder   **COUNTRY:** Romania   **DOB:** 23/01/2003

Rus joined Coventry City from Southampton in July 2021. Last season, Marco was an influential member of the Under-21s group who made it to the Birmingham Senior Cup final, wearing the captain's armband on multiple occasions.

He also spent time away from City, enjoying loan spells with Hereford and Chorley, gaining some valuable minutes in the National League North.

19

Kasey PALMER
45

POSITION: Midfielder   **COUNTRY:** Jamaica   **DOB:** 09/11/1996

Kasey Palmer joined the Sky Blues from Bristol City ahead of the 2022/23 season. Palmer came through the ranks at Chelsea, enjoying loan spells away from Stamford Bridge in the Championship and then the Premier League with Huddersfield Town between 2016 and 2017, after winning the Championship Play-Off final with the Terriers. Kasey played a very important role in his first season making 32 appearances including one in the Play-Off final at Wembley.

Evan EGHOSA
47

POSITION: Midfielder   **COUNTRY:** England   **DOB:** 05/08/2005

Versatile midfielder Eghosa signed his first professional contract in the Summer of 2023. He had an impressive season for the Under-21s last time out, during which he established himself as an important player in John Dempster's side that reached the final of the Birmingham Senior Cup. His impressive 2022/23 campaign saw him rewarded with a pre-season spent training and playing alongside senior stars at the Sky Blue Lodge and on tour in Portugal, before featuring during pre-season friendlies too.

Justin
OBIKWU

49

POSITION: Striker   COUNTRY: England   DOB: 06/05/2004

Obikwu signed his first professional contract in July 2023. Obikwu found the back of the net in City's first pre-season fixture against Forest Green Rovers, adding the fourth in a 4-0 win. The 19-year-old trained with the first team during pre-season, joining Mark Robins' side out in Portugal on tour. Last season, Obikwu enjoyed a breakthrough campaign with the Under-21s side, featuring on a regular basis throughout the campaign and scoring goals, helping fire City to the Birmingham Senior Cup final.

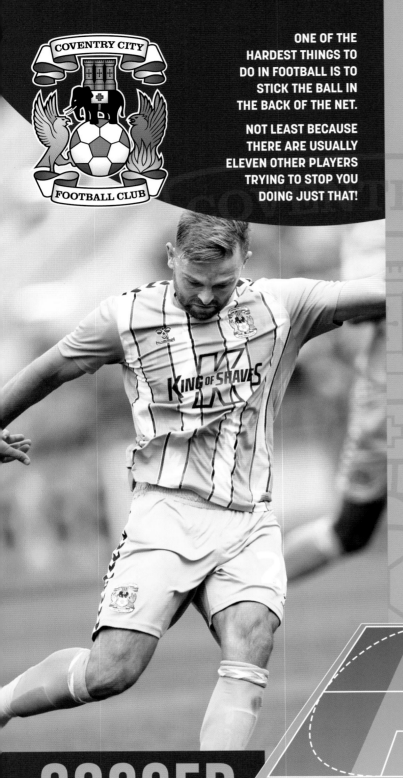

SHOOTING
FROM DISTANCE

Good service is obviously important, and a good understanding with your striking partner is also vital, but when it comes to spectacular strikes, practice is the key to hitting a consistently accurate and powerful shot and to developing the timing and power required.

EXERCISE

A small-sided pitch is set up with two 18-yard boxes put together, but the corners of the pitch are cut off as shown in the diagram. There are five players per team, including goalkeepers, but only one player is allowed in the opponent's half.

The aim of the drill is to work a shooting opportunity when you have the ball, with the likely chance being to shoot from outside your opponent's penalty area, from distance. The teams take it in turns to release the ball into play from their own 'keeper - usually by rolling out to an unmarked player.

18 YDS

SOCCER
SKILLS

KEY FACTORS

1. **Attitude to shooting - be positive, have a go!**
2. **Technique - use laces, hit through the ball.**
3. **Do not sacrifice accuracy for power.**
4. **Wide angle shooting - aim for the far post.**
5. **Always follow up for rebounds!**

The size of the pitch can be reduced for younger players, and it should be noted that these junior players should also be practicing with a size 4 or even a size 3 ball, depending on their age.

KYLE
McFADZEAN

5

COVENTRY CITY
FOOTBALL CLUB

23

COVENTRY CITY
WOMEN & GIRLS FC

Coventry City Women & Girls FC are one of the largest female only, grassroots clubs in the West Midlands

We currently 18 teams registered with the Football Association, ranging from girls teams at Under 9s all the way through to our Women's First Team for the 2023/24 season, developing a CLEAR pathway for girls and women.

We have been investing in female football since 1991. This club is run by volunteers that work tirelessly to raise funds, manage teams and ensure all FA standards are met.

We are honoured to work alongside CCFC and Sky Blues in The Community. As a club we not only strive to improve players ability, but we invest heavily in our managers and coaches to increase their coaching skills through courses held by Birmingham FA.

The 2022-23 season had huge success for the club with many teams finishing in the top three in their league, leading to promotion. Many tournaments have been won and there was a proud moment in retaining the winners title at the Aces National tournament for the second year.

There are no limits. There has never been a better time to get involved with the growing game for females, empowering girls with self-esteem and confidence - shaping leaders for the future!

We thank everyone for their hard work and support, including club ambassadors Dave Bennett and Dave Busst.

We are very privileged to be a part of Coventry City and all wear the badge with pride.

OUR ANNUAL CLUB DAY AT COVENTRY BUILDING SOCIETY ARENA - AN AMAZING DAY FOR ALL INVOLVED.
THE GIRLS GET SO EXCITED TO WALK ROUND THE PITCH AND WISH THAT ONE DAY THEY CAN PLAY ON A PITCH LIKE THIS AND IN FRONT OF A BIG CROWD.

THE GIRLS VISIT ST GEORGE'S PARK

PRE-SEASON VISITING INTERNATIONAL TEAMS FROM DUBAI, HONG KONG AND USA

25

DAZZLING DEFENDERS

BRIAN KILCLINE, PHIL BABB AND ELLIOTT WARD WERE ALL OUTSTANDING DEFENDERS FOR THE SKY BLUES AND CONTINUING THAT TRADITION IS THE EVER-RELIABLE KYLE MCFADZEAN.

Phil Babb proved to be a shrewd £500,000 signing from Bradford City during the summer of 1992, and his Sky Blues debut coincided with the club's first Premier League fixture at home to Middlesbrough on the opening day of the 1992/93 season.

Babb had a great turn of pace and was always alert to danger, he was comfortable in possession and had the ability to play at left-back as well as his preferred position as a central defender.

A string of highly-polished performances at the heart of the City defence won him international recognition with the Republic of Ireland. In September 1994, the Sky Blues sold Babb to Liverpool for £3.6m which made him the most expensive defender in Britain at the time.

Brian Kilcline joined the Sky Blues from Notts County in June 1984 and swiftly established a fine centre-back pairing with Trevor Peake.

A commanding and no-nonsense central defender, Kilcline was an unmistakable character with his trademark long hair and moustache. He had fantastic ability in the air and was City's regular penalty taker too.

He captained Coventry City in the club's finest hour as the Sky Blues defeated Tottenham Hotspur at Wembley in 1987 to win the FA Cup for the first time in the club's history. He later played for Oldham Athletic, Newcastle United, Swindon Town, Mansfield Town and Halifax Town. However, he made more league appearances for Coventry than any of his other six clubs.

BRIAN KILCLINE

DATE OF BIRTH: 7 May 1962

PLACE OF BIRTH: Nottingham

NATIONALITY: English

SKY BLUES APPEARANCES: 213

SKY BLUES GOALS: 35

SKY BLUES DEBUT: 25 August 1984
Aston Villa 1-0 Coventry City (First Division)

PHIL BABB

DATE OF BIRTH: 30 November 1970

PLACE OF BIRTH: Lambeth

NATIONALITY: Irish

SKY BLUES APPEARANCES: 84

SKY BLUES GOALS: 4

SKY BLUES DEBUT: 15 August 1992
Coventry City 2-1 Middlesbrough (Premier League)

Elliott Ward arrived at Coventry City ahead of the 2006/07 season when he completed a £1m transfer from West Ham United.

Signed by boss Micky Adams, Ward was a talented and confident young central defender who had sampled first-team football at Championship and Premier League level with the Hammers. He had also gained vital experience with loan spells at Bristol Rovers and Plymouth Argyle.

Ward soon became a mainstay of the Sky Blues' defence over the following three seasons with his brave and committed performances winning him plenty of plaudits. Much like Brian Kilcline before him, Ward was also charged with penalty taking responsibilities for the Sky Blues.

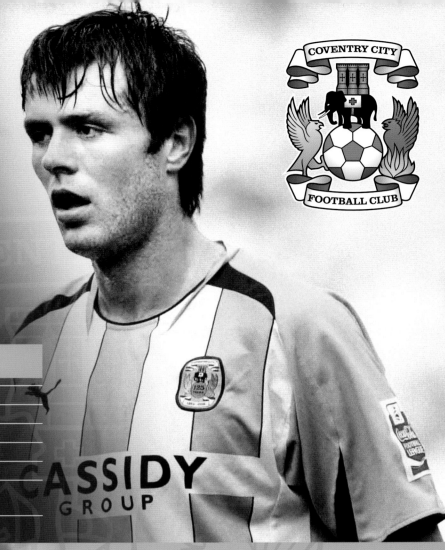

ELLIOTT WARD

DATE OF BIRTH:	19 January 1985
PLACE OF BIRTH:	Harrow
NATIONALITY:	English
SKY BLUES APPEARANCES:	126
SKY BLUES GOALS:	16
SKY BLUES DEBUT:	6 August 2006

Coventry City 2-1 Sunderland (Championship)

KYLE McFADZEAN

DATE OF BIRTH:	20 February 1987
PLACE OF BIRTH:	Sheffield
NATIONALITY:	English
SKY BLUES APPEARANCES:	156*
SKY BLUES GOALS:	8*
SKY BLUES DEBUT:	3 August 2019

Coventry City 1-0 Southend United (League One)

*AS AT THE END OF THE 2022/23 SEASON

Kyle McFadzean brings a wealth of experience to the current Coventry side and has become a real leader of the team's defensive unit following his 2019 arrival from Burton Albion.

McFadzean played a vital role in helping the Sky Blues to the League One title in his first season at the club. He then showed no problem in stepping up to the challenge of Championship football and was a tower of strength as Mark Robins' men established themselves back in the second tier.

With over 150 Coventry City appearances to his name, McFadzean is a well-respected character both on and off the pitch and the club's current vice-captain.

TATSUHIRO
SAKAMOTO

7

FOOTY PHRASES

ALL OF THESE FOOTY PHRASES ARE HIDDEN IN THE GRID, EXCEPT FOR ONE ...BUT CAN YOU WORK OUT WHICH ONE?

ANSWERS ON PAGE 62

```
C A E S W Y V V B H U G N U R Y M M U D
V U Q I D E R B Y D A Y O L U R T S S U
K F A D J L G T X T F C B E I A K C F P
I B H E O T L P Z R V N M W O J I R Y A
C M O F F S I D E R U L E E D S P E Y H
M E R U E I J R D E D A Q G S H L A X C
R X E R N H A T T R I C K O I L A M R T
E I Y O W S L S N O W R S O Z Y E Y A
D C A A Z L W S J K T K Y V K B M R T M
A A L P X A U Y H M I D F I E D A R O E
E N P T K N F W G C P L J K A M K N L H
H W E J A I L O K H A O F O H I E C G T
G A M E O F T W O H A L V E S T R N U F
N V A I A H E S L F J D U A O I U O T O
I E G B I C L A S S A C T U P F G E V N
V D G O A E E U C K S S C Y W U L Q L A
I R I R Q G M N S A C H G H D O S F G M
D V B A C K O F T H E N E T Z P X B N A
```

Back of the Net
Big Game Player
Brace
Class Act
Derby Day
Diving Header
Dugout
Dummy Run
Final Whistle
Game of Two Halves
Half Volley
Hat-trick
Keepie Uppie
Man of the Match
Mexican Wave
Offside Rule
One-touch
Playmaker
Scissor Kick
Screamer

PLAYER
OF THE SEASON

Midfield maestro Gustavo Hamer was voted Coventry City's Player of the Year for the 2022/23 season.

Following the annual supporters' poll, Hamer collected the award for the second consecutive season following a string of sensational performances throughout a memorable campaign as the Sky Blues found themselves within touching distance of the Premier League.

Hamer's outstanding performances were a key factor in the club's drive to the end-of-season Play-Offs and the Wembley final with Luton Town. As well as being the creative force in engineering opportunities for teammates, Hamer weighed in with nine Championship goals as Mark Robins' men secured a fifth-place finish.

In a close-fought Play-Off semi-final against Middlesbrough, it was the Sky Blues, who in Hamer, just had that little bit of extra guile and class to win a place in the Wembley final. His memorable winning goal at the Riverside Stadium took his tally for the season into double figures, but the Dutch star was not finished yet.

Hamer of course netted the Sky Blues' second-half equaliser against the Hatters at Wembley and all Coventry fans will wonder just what might have been had their main man not have been forced to come off injured with ten minutes remaining.

A class act and much valued member of the City squad, 26-year-old Hamer made 45 appearances in all competitions in 2022/23 and was clearly a deserved winner of the Player of the Year accolade.

YOUNG PLAYER OF THE SEASON

Manchester City loanee Callum Doyle enjoyed an exceptional 2022/23 with the Sky Blues and ended the campaign with the club's Young Player of the Year award.

Presented to a player aged under 23 and chosen by the club's coaching staff, Doyle who turns 20 in October 2023 was a unanimous choice for the award.

Almost ever-present during a highly successful season at the Coventry Arena, Doyle featured in 46 matches for the Sky Blues last season when his assured performances made a lasting impression on the club's supporters.

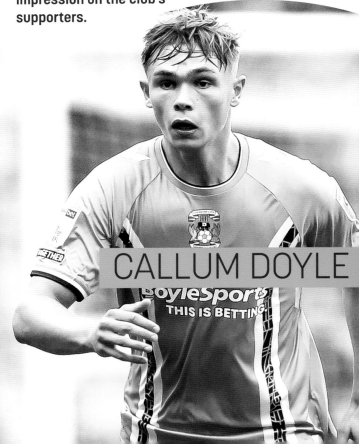

CALLUM DOYLE

GUSTAVO HAMER

COVENTRY CITY FOOTBALL CLUB

SOCCER SKILLS

THE WALL PASS

With teams being very organised in modern football, it can be very difficult to break them down and create scoring opportunities. One of the best ways to achieve this is by using the 'wall pass', otherwise known as the quick one-two.

EXERCISE

In a non-pressurised situation, involving four players, A carries the ball forward towards a static defender (in this case a cone) and before reaching the defender, plays the ball to B before running around the opposite side to receive the one-touch return pass. A then delivers the ball safely to C who then repeats the exercise returning the ball to D, and in this way the exercise continues. Eventually a defender can be used to make the exercise more challenging, with all players being rotated every few minutes.

The exercise can progress into a five-a-side game, the diagram below shows how additional players (W) on the touchline can be used as 'walls' with just one touch available to help the man in possession of the ball.

Each touchline player can move up and down the touchline, but not enter the pitch - they can also play for either team.

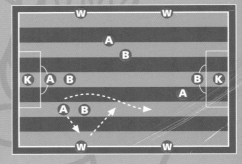

KEY FACTORS

1. Look to commit the defender before passing - do not play the ball too early.
2. Pass the ball firmly and to feet.
3. Accelerate past defender after passing.
4. Receiver (B) make themselves available for the pass.
5. B delivers a return pass, weighted correctly, into space.

If done correctly, this is a tactic which is extremely difficult to stop, but needs teamwork and communication between the two attacking players.

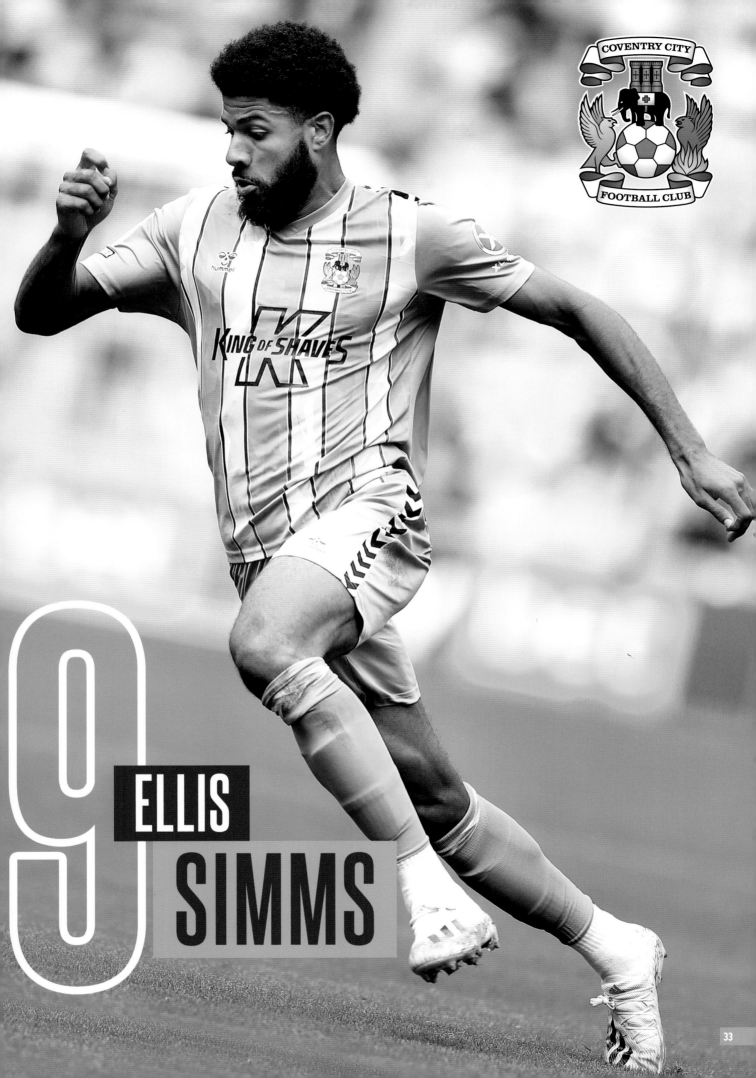

9

ELLIS
SIMMS

A-Z

ARE YOU READY TO TACKLE OUR A-Z FOOTBALL QUIZ?

THE SIMPLE RULE IS THAT THE ANSWERS RUN THROUGH THE 26 LETTERS OF THE ALPHABET.

A

What nationality is Watford goalkeeper Daniel Bachmann?

A

B

Which team won the Sky Bet Championship title in 2022/23?

B

C

Which Premier League club reappointed their former manager as interim boss in March 2023?

C

D

Which League One side play their home matches at Pride Park?

D

E

What nationality is Liverpool's sensational striker Mohamed Salah?

E

F

Which country knocked England out of the FIFA World Cup finals in 2022?

F

G

Which famous football ground is due to host its final fixture in 2024?

G

K

What is the name of Premier League new boys Luton Town's home ground?

K

L

Can you name the Ipswich Town striker who netted 17 League One goals in the Tractor Boys' 2022/23 promotion-winning season?

L

M

Which Championship club boasted the division's top scorer in 2022/23?

M

H
Which club did Neil Warnock lead to Championship survival in 2022/23?

H

I
Which country did England defeat 6-2 in their opening game of the FIFA 2022 World Cup finals?

I

J
Aston Villa winger Leon Bailey plays internationally for which country?

J

ANSWERS ON PAGE 62

Q Can you name the country that hosted the FIFA 2022 World Cup finals?

Q

R Which Spanish side did Manchester City defeat in last season's UEFA Champions League semi-final?

R

S Which team knocked Premier League champions Manchester City out of the Carabao Cup last season?

S

N

What nationality is Manchester City's ace marksman Erling Haaland?

N

O Can you name the former Premier League team that will compete in the National League in 2023/24?

O

P Which international striker ended five seasons with Norwich City in May 2023?

P

T **Which full-back left Huddersfield Town to join Nottingham Forest ahead of their return to the Premier League in the summer of 2022?**

T

X Can you name the Portuguese international defender who played in the Premier League with Everton, Liverpool & Middlesbrough?

X

U Can you name Brighton's German forward who joined the Seagulls in January 2022?

U

Y At which club did Leeds United's Luke Ayling make his league debut?

Y

V Can you name the former England striker who has hit over 100 Premier League goals for Leicester City?

V

W Can you name the goalkeeper who got his name on the scoresheet last season in a Championship fixture?

W

Z Which Dutch international midfielder played Premier League football for Chelsea, Middlesbrough and Liverpool in the 2000s?

Z

A-Z

PART TWO

ANSWERS ON PAGE 62

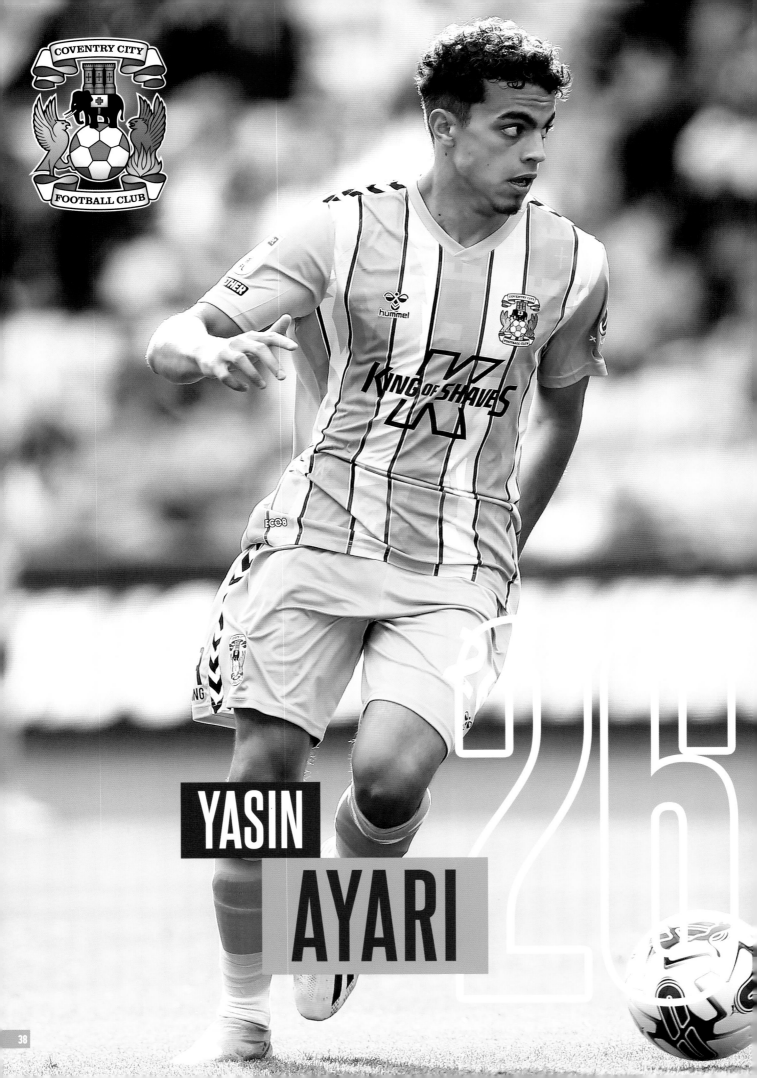

YASIN
AYARI

38

DESIGN A FOOTY BOOT

Design a brilliant new footy boot for the Sky Blues squad!

MIDFIELD
MAESTROS

STEVE SEDGLEY, GARY McALLISTER AND JAMES MADDISON ALL PROVIDED A CREATIVE PRESENCE IN THE COVENTRY CITY MIDFIELD. CONTINUING THAT FINE TRADITION IS THE SKY BLUES MIDFIELD PLAYMAKER CALLUM O'HARE.

Gary McAllister was already an experienced Scottish international when he joined the Sky Blues from Leeds United in a £3m deal ahead of the club's 1996/97 Premier League campaign.

As Coventry City captain, McAllister helped inspire the team to a remarkable top-flight survival in his first season at the club including a never-to-be-forgotten final day victory away to Tottenham Hotspur.

A top-quality midfield technician, who orchestrated play and was the brains behind many set-play situations, McAllister spent four seasons with the club before going on to enjoy success with Liverpool. In 2002 he returned to the Sky Blues as player-manager.

Steve Sedgley progressed through the club's youth ranks and was given his chance to shine at first-team level as a teenager when he debuted in a 2-1 First Division victory over Arsenal at Highfield Road in 1986.

The 1986/87 season certainly proved to be a breakthrough campaign for Sedgley who made 32 appearances in all competitions and ended the season with an FA Cup winners' medal having been an unused substitute in the Sky Blues' Wembley victory over Tottenham Hotspur.

Across a three-season period as an energic and skilful midfielder, Sedgley made over a century of first-team appearances for Coventry before securing a £750,000 switch to Tottenham in the summer of 1989. In 1991, he won his second FA Cup winners' medal having helped Spurs overcome Nottingham Forest in the showpiece final.

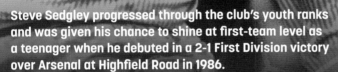

STEVE SEDGLEY

DATE OF BIRTH:	26 May 1968
PLACE OF BIRTH:	Enfield
NATIONALITY:	English
SKY BLUES APPEARANCES:	103
SKY BLUES GOALS:	5
SKY BLUES DEBUT:	26 August 1986

Coventry City 2-1 Arsenal (First Division)

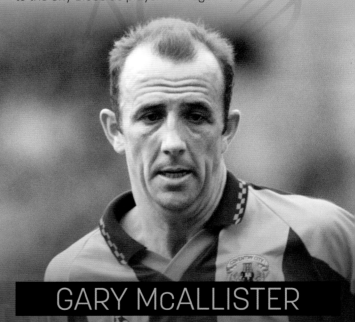

GARY McALLISTER

DATE OF BIRTH:	25 December 1964
PLACE OF BIRTH:	Motherwell
NATIONALITY:	Scottish
SKY BLUES APPEARANCES:	200
SKY BLUES GOALS:	38
SKY BLUES DEBUT:	17 August 1996

Coventry City 0-3 Nottingham Forest (Premier League)

James Maddison is widely regarded as the best player to emerge through the Coventry City Academy.

An immensely talented midfielder, Maddison arrived on the Sky Blues' first-team scene as a teenager in 2014. His performances saw the scouts flooding to watch and in January 2016 he was snapped up by then-Premier League Norwich City.

After loan spells back with the Sky Blues and then north of the border with Aberdeen, he became a real class act in the Norwich City midfield and secured a reported £20m move to Leicester City in the summer of 2018. An FA Cup winner with the Foxes, Maddison's Leicester form was rewarded with full international honours with England and a recent move to Tottenham Hotspur.

JAMES MADDISON

DATE OF BIRTH:	23 November 1996
PLACE OF BIRTH:	Coventry
NATIONALITY:	English
SKY BLUES APPEARANCES:	42
SKY BLUES GOALS:	5
SKY BLUES DEBUT:	13 August 2014

Coventry City 1-2 Cardiff City (League Cup)

CALLUM O'HARE

DATE OF BIRTH:	1 May 1998
PLACE OF BIRTH:	Solihull
NATIONALITY:	English
SKY BLUES APPEARANCES:	108*
SKY BLUES GOALS:	8*
SKY BLUES DEBUT:	24 August 2019

Coventry City 1-0 Gillingham (League One)

*AS AT THE END OF THE 2022/23 SEASON

Callum O'Hare starred on loan for Coventry City in the 2019/20 League One title-winning season. Following his release by Aston Villa in the summer of 2020 he then joined the Sky Blues on a permanent basis.

Blessed with exceptional close control and the ability to create chances for himself or teammates, O'Hare can get supporters up and out of their seats with moments of breathtaking trickery in attacking areas.

While terrible bad luck with injuries has hampered his time at the club, there is no disputing the Sky Blues are at their best with a fit and firing O'Hare in the team. Mark Robins and all at the Coventry Arena will be hopeful of seeing O'Hare back at his match-winning best this season.

CLASSIC FAN'TASTIC

Sky Blue Sam is hiding in the crowd in five different places as Coventry City fans celebrate winning the FA Cup in 1987.

Can you find all five? ANSWERS ON PAGE 62

MILAN
VAN EWIJK

27

14

BEN
SHEAF

GOAL
OF THE SEASON

Hamer then turned from creator to scorer as he settled the fixture in Coventry's favour with a sensational solo effort after 65 minutes. Skipping his way past two men and into the opposition's penalty area he then sent a fabulous curling right-foot shot past home 'keeper Josef Bursik and into the bottom corner to the delight of the travelling Sky Blue Army who celebrated both a wonder-goal and a third consecutive Championship victory.

The goal was Hamer second of an eleven-goal campaign and had voting have taken place after the Play-Offs then surely his smartly executed winner against Middlesbrough in the Play-Off semi-final would have been another contender for Coventry City's 2022/23 Goal of the Season award.

The Sky Blues' end-of-season awards ceremony provided a double celebration for ace midfielder Gustavo Hamer who followed up his Player of the Year award with the club's Goal of the Season title too.

It was the Brazil-born Dutchman's second-half stunner in the 2-0 win away to Stoke City in October 2022 that was judged to have been the Sky Blues' top strike from the 2022/23 campaign.

The match marked Hamer's first start in over a month after the 26-year-old had been forced to serve a four-match ban following two early-season dismissals.

Unsurprisingly with Hamer in the side, the Sky Blues looked a class act and this win really was all about Hamer's ability to create and score goals for Mark Robins' team.

Six minutes into the second half and Coventry opened the scoring when Hamer split the Potters' defence with a perfect pass into the left channel that set Jamie Allen free to run on and rifle the ball home.

GUSTAVO HAMER

V STOKE CITY

BEHIND THE BADGE

A

B

C

48

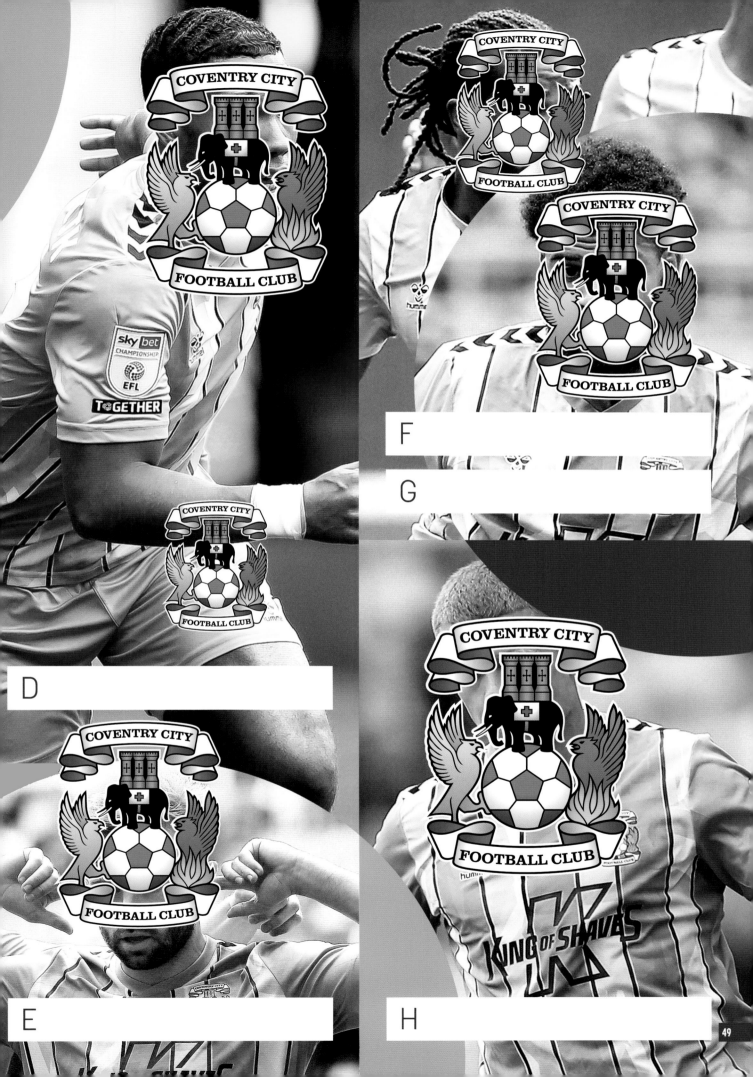

D

E

F

G

H

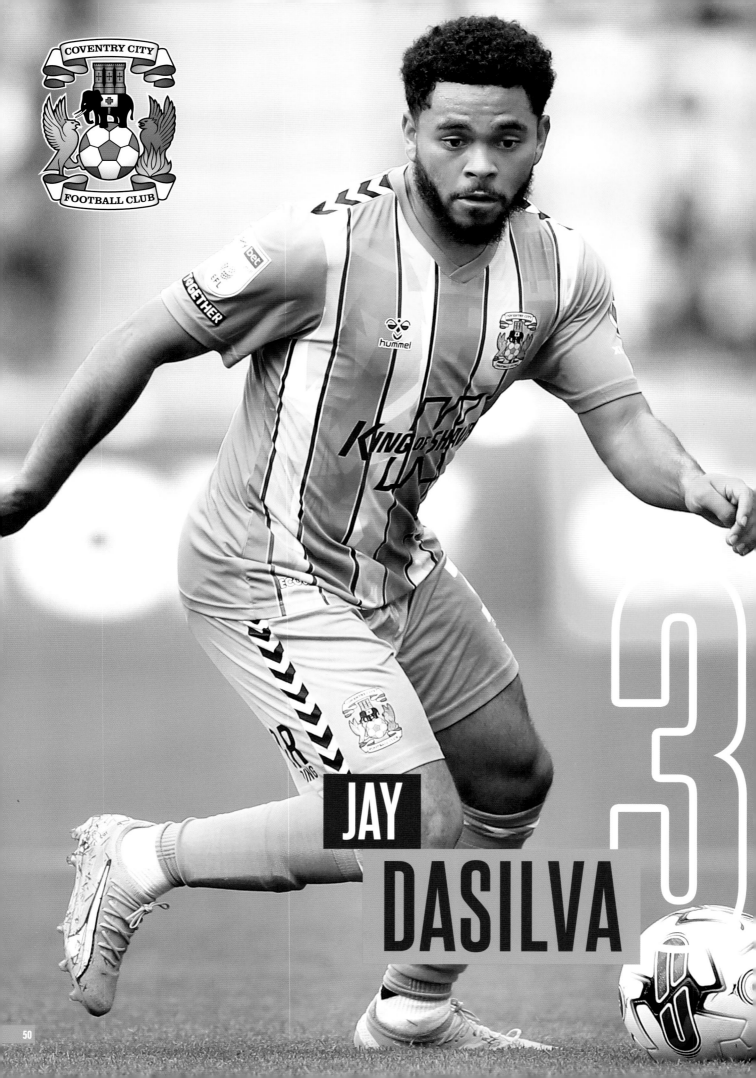

JAY
DASILVA
3

TRUE
COLOURS

HAVE FUN COLOURING
IN THIS PICTURE
OF SKY BLUES STAR
JAY DASILVA

STUNNING
STRIKERS

CYRILLE REGIS, DION DUBLIN AND DARREN HUCKERBY WERE ALL ACE MARKSMEN FOR THE SKY BLUES. LOOKING TO FOLLOW IN THEIR FOOTSTEPS IS CURRENT COVENTRY STRIKER MATT GODDEN.

Dion Dublin won the adulation of the Highfield Road faithful as consistent goalscorer for Coventry City who led the line superbly though his time at the club.

Much like Cyrille Regis, Dublin was a powerful front-man who embraced the responsibility of being Coventry's go to man for goals. His physical presence ensured that any central defender who was challenged with the task of marking him would certainly have known they had been in a game.

A great leader and big personality during his time at Coventry, the club paid £2m to sign him from Manchester United in September 1994 and he repaid that fee by establishing himself as one of the Premier League's most feared strikers in the late '90s.

Cyrille Regis provided a real physical presence and touch of know-how to the Coventry City attack and played a vital part in the club's 1987 FA Cup triumph at Wembley.

Regis was a natural goalscorer who was a threat to the opposition either in the air or on the deck. An experienced striker, he arrived at Highfield Road in 1984 following a lengthy spell with Midlands rivals West Bromwich Albion. The £250,000 transfer fee proved to be something of a bargain as Regis' performances won him cult status with the Coventry City supporters.

His form at Highfield Road saw him earn a return to the full England squad in 1987 as he won his fifth and final England cap.

CYRILLE REGIS

DATE OF BIRTH:	9 February 1958
PLACE OF BIRTH:	Maripasoula, French Guiana
NATIONALITY:	English
SKY BLUES APPEARANCES:	282
SKY BLUES GOALS:	61
SKY BLUES DEBUT:	13 October 1984

Coventry City 1-1 Newcastle United (First Division)

DION DUBLIN

DATE OF BIRTH:	22 April 1969
PLACE OF BIRTH:	Leicester
NATIONALITY:	English
SKY BLUES APPEARANCES:	171
SKY BLUES GOALS:	72
SKY BLUES DEBUT:	10 September 1994

Queens Park Rangers 2-2 Coventry City (First Division)

Darren Huckerby was blessed with electric pace and supreme confidence and those two attributes made him a real match-winner throughout his Coventry City career.

Often paired with Dion Dublin or Noel Whelan, Huckerby was one of the most exciting players to grace the Coventry City forward line. Fondly remembered by the Sky Blues' fans for his dazzling run and winning goal in a fantastic 3-2 Premier League victory over Manchester United at Highfield Road in December 1997, Huckerby played a key role in the team's eleventh place top-flight finish that season.

His form for the Sky Blues made him one of the most highly rated talents in the Premier League and in 1999 he was sold to big spending Leeds United for a £6m fee.

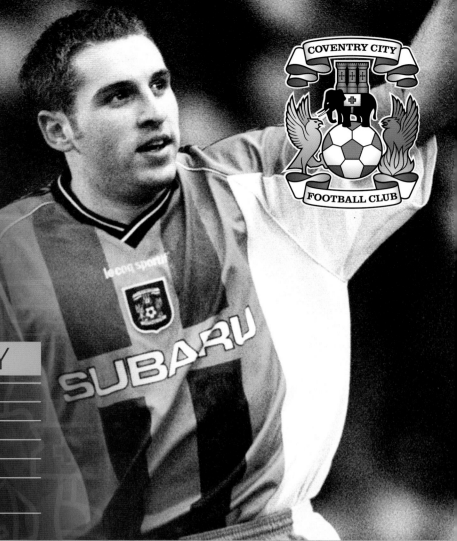

DARREN HUCKERBY

DATE OF BIRTH:	23 April 1976
PLACE OF BIRTH:	Nottingham
NATIONALITY:	English
SKY BLUES APPEARANCES:	109
SKY BLUES GOALS:	34
SKY BLUES DEBUT:	23 November 1996

Coventry City 1-2 Aston Villa (Premier League)

MATT GODDEN

DATE OF BIRTH:	29 July 1991
PLACE OF BIRTH:	Canterbury
NATIONALITY:	English
SKY BLUES APPEARANCES:	115*
SKY BLUES GOALS:	41*
SKY BLUES DEBUT:	10 August 2019

Bolton Wanderers 0-0 Coventry City (League One)

*AS AT THE END OF THE 2022/23 SEASON

Matt Godden netted 14 goals in his first season with the Sky Blues as the club were promoted as League One champions in 2019/20 and his goals have continued to make City a major force at Championship level.

A live-wire striker who always appears alert when in and around the opposition's penalty area, Godden began his career with Scunthorpe United and joined the Sky Blues in 2019 following highly impressive scoring spells with Stevenage and Peterborough United.

He netted eight Championship goals at the Sky Blues reached the 2022/23 Play-Off final at Wembley and began the current campaign in fine form with three goals in his first four outings of the season.

REWIND

Coventry City 2
Sunderland 1

SKY BET CHAMPIONSHIP · FEBRUARY 25, 2023

Victory over fellow Play-Off hopefuls Sunderland at the Arena in February saw the Sky Blues make it three consecutive Championship victories as Mark Robins' men began their climb up the Championship table.

Leading marksman Viktor Gyökeres turned from scorer to provider to tee-up Jamie Allen for a 25th-minute opener and then netted his 16th goal of the season to double the Sky Blues' lead after 89 minutes.

Although Amad Diallo reduced the arrears in injury-time, the hosts saw the game out for an important three points and victory over former Coventry boss Tony Mowbray.

Huddersfield Town 0
Coventry City 4

SKY BET CHAMPIONSHIP · MARCH 4, 2023

The Sky Blues got the month of March off to the best possible start with an emphatic victory over struggling Huddersfield Town at the John Smith's Stadium.

Leading 1-0 at the break thanks to Viktor Gyökeres' 31st-minute opener, Coventry made a sensational start to the second-half with two goals in 14 minutes to take the game away from the Terriers.

Gustavo Hamer doubled the lead on 55 before Gyökeres added his second and the Sky Blues' third after 59 minutes action. Substitute Tyler Walker scored a fourth in the final minute as Coventry made it four wins from five matches.

Coventry City 2
Birmingham City 0

SKY BET CHAMPIONSHIP · APRIL 29, 2023

Goals at the beginning and end of the first-half gave the Sky Blues another vital three points as they closed in on a top-six finish.

In front of a crowd of over 30,000 - City got off to the best possible start when Josh Eccles fired home his first senior goal to give the side a third-minute lead. Then just three minutes before the break Viktor Gyökeres bagged his 22nd goal of the season from the penalty spot. Victory over their Midlands rivals saw the Sky Blues head into their final fixture with their Play-Off hopes firmly in their own hands.

FAST FORWARD

Leicester City (HOME)

SKY BET CHAMPIONSHIP · JANUARY 13, 2024

After kicking-off the new season away to local rivals Leicester City, the Sky Blues will host the Foxes on January 13 in one of the most eagerly anticipated home games of the season.

Since last visiting the Arena for a Championship fixture in August 2011, Leicester City have enjoyed the most successful period in the club's history with the Foxes crowned Premier League champions in 2016 and FA Cup winners in 2021.

Relegated from the top flight at the end of last season, Leicester will be among the favourites for an instant return to the Premier League.

Leeds United (HOME)

SKY BET CHAMPIONSHIP · APRIL 6, 2024

Just like Leicester City, Leeds United were also relegated from the Premier League last season and will be strongly fancied to mount a serious bid for promotion back to the top flight at the first time of asking.

The Elland Road club are now under the management of former Norwich City manager Daniel Farke. The German won the Championship title twice with the Canaries he will be going in search of a hat-trick of second tier titles in 2023/34.

Leeds will provide our second opponents in the busy month of April and the match at the Arena on April 6 certainly appears one not to miss.

Southampton (AWAY)

SKY BET CHAMPIONSHIP · APRIL 9, 2024

As the season reaches its business end, the Sky Blues will head to the Southampton for a league match for the first time since April 2012.

The Saints complete the trio of teams relegated from the Premier League in 2022/23 and are sure to provide a tough challenge for Mark Robins' men when we travel to St Mary's Stadium just three days after hosting Leeds United.

Southampton are another club who made a managerial change in the summer of 2023 with former MK Dons and Swansea City head coach Russell Martin being the man appointed to spearhead the Saints' promotion ambitions.

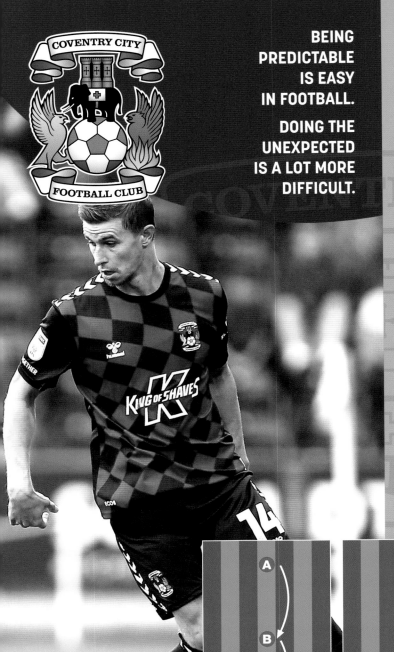

TURNING
WITH THE BALL

One of the biggest problems a defence can have to deal with is when a skilful player is prepared to turn with the ball and run at them, committing a key defender into making a challenge. Because football today is so fast and space so precious, this is becoming a rare skill.

EXERCISE 1

In an area 20m x 10m, A plays the ball into B who turns, and with two touches maximum plays the ball into C. C controls and reverses the process. After a few minutes the middleman is changed.

As you progress, a defender is brought in to oppose B, and is initially encouraged to play a 'passive' role. B has to turn and play the ball to C who is allowed to move along the baseline.

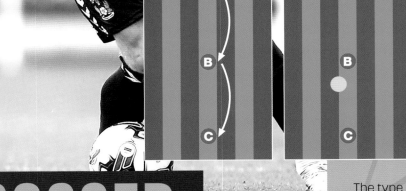

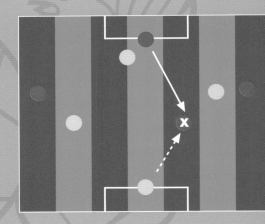

The type of turns can vary. Players should be encouraged to use the outside of the foot, inside of the foot, with feint and disguise to make space for the turn.

EXERCISE 2

As the players grow in confidence, you can move forward to a small-sided game. In this example of a 4-a-side practice match, X has made space for himself to turn with the ball, by coming off his defender at an angle.

By doing this he can see that the defender has not tracked him, and therefore has the awareness to turn and attack.

Matches at the top level are won and lost by pieces of skill such as this, so players have to be brave enough to go in search of the ball, and turn in tight situations.

SOCCER
SKILLS

24

MATT
GODDEN

HIGH FIVES

HOW GOOD IS YOUR SKY BLUES KNOWLEDGE?

PUT YOUR MEMORY TO THE TEST WITH OUR HIGH FIVES QUIZ

1. Across the previous five seasons, who have been Coventry's leading league scorers?

1. _____
2. _____
3. _____
4. _____
5. _____

2. Can you name Coventry's last five FA Cup opponents ahead of the 2023/24 season?

1. _____
2. _____
3. _____
4. _____
5. _____

3. Prior to Mark Robins, who were the club's last five permanent managers?

1. _____
2. _____
3. _____
4. _____
5. _____

4. Can you name the Sky Blues' last five EFL Cup opponents as at the end of 2022/23?

1. _____
2. _____
3. _____
4. _____
5. _____

5. Can you recall the Sky Blues' final league position from each of the last five seasons?

1.
2.
3.
4.
5.

8. Can you recall the score and season from the last five derby wins over Leicester City?

1.
2.
3.
4.
5.

6. Which members of the Coventry squad started the most league games last season?

1.
2.
3.
4.
5.

9. Can you remember Coventry's last five Championship victories from last season?

1.
2.
3.
4.
5.

7. Can you recall these players' squad numbers from the 2022/23 season?

1. Callum O'Hare
2. Ben Sheaf
3. Ben Wilson
4. Michael Rose
5. Josh Eccles

10. Can you recall the club's end of season points tally from the last five seasons?

1.
2.
3.
4.
5.

ANSWERS ON PAGE 62

SENSATIONAL STOPPERS

STEVE OGRIZOVIC, MAGNUS HEDMAN AND KEIREN WESTWOOD WERE ALL TOP-CLASS 'KEEPERS FOR COVENTRY CITY. CONTINUING THAT PROUD TREND IS CURRENT SKY BLUES NO.1 BEN WILSON.

Magnus Hedman was a Swedish international who starred between the posts for the Sky Blues and helped the club secure an eleventh place Premier League finish in 1997/98.

An athletic 'keeper with great reflex skills and superb anticipation of danger, Hedman kept a clean sheet on his Sky Blues' debut in a memorable 4-0 victory over Tottenham Hotspur in December 1997.

His exceptional club form saw him establish himself as first choice 'keeper for both club and country. He made 44 of his 58 international appearances for Sweden while plying his trade at Highfield Road and that makes him the Sky Blues' most capped player.

Steve Ogrizovic is our record appearance maker who represented Coventry City across 16 seasons and kept goal in the club's historic 1987 FA Cup final victory over Tottenham Hotspur at Wembley.

Signed from Shrewsbury Town for £72,500 in 1984, 'Big Oggy' played a vital role in many of the club's great escape acts as the Sky Blues maintained top-flight status.

A true Coventry City legend, one of many club records he holds saw him play 209 consecutive league games and he even scored in a 2-2 draw away to Sheffield Wednesday in 1986. After hanging up his gloves he then spent 20 years on the coaching staff as reserve team manager, goalkeeper coach and even caretaker manager.

STEVE OGRIZOVIC

DATE OF BIRTH:	12 September 1957
PLACE OF BIRTH:	Mansfield
NATIONALITY:	English
SKY BLUES APPEARANCES:	601
SKY BLUES GOALS:	1
SKY BLUES DEBUT:	25 August 1984

Aston Vila 1-0 Coventry City (First Division)

MAGNUS HEDMAN

DATE OF BIRTH:	19 March 1973
PLACE OF BIRTH:	Huddinge, Sweden
NATIONALITY:	Swedish
SKY BLUES APPEARANCES:	151
SKY BLUES GOALS:	0
SKY BLUES DEBUT:	13 December 1997

Coventry City 4-0 Tottenham Hotspur (Premier League)

Keiren Westwood proved to be an extremely reliable last line of defence for the Sky Blues across three seasons at the Coventry Arena.

Recruited from Carlisle United in the summer of 2008, Westwood enjoyed an impressive and ever-present debut Championship campaign for Coventry in 2008/09. His form was rewarded with a place in the Championship PFA Team of the Year for 2009.

An exceptional one-on-one stopper, Westwood's Coventry club form won him international recognition with the Republic of Ireland and in his second season with the club he was voted Player of the Season for 2009/10 by the supporters. In June 2011 he joined Premier League Sunderland and later played for Sheffield Wednesday and Queens Park Rangers.

KEIREN WESTWOOD

DATE OF BIRTH: 23 October 1984

PLACE OF BIRTH: Manchester

NATIONALITY: English

SKY BLUES APPEARANCES: 138

SKY BLUES GOALS: 0

SKY BLUES DEBUT: 9 August 2008
Coventry City 2-1 Norwich City (Premier League)

BEN WILSON

DATE OF BIRTH: 9 August 1992

PLACE OF BIRTH: Stanley

NATIONALITY: English

SKY BLUES APPEARANCES: 90*

SKY BLUES GOALS: 1*

SKY BLUES DEBUT: 13 August 2019
Coventry City 4-1 Exeter City (League Cup)

*AS AT THE END OF THE 2022/23 SEASON

Ben Wilson joined the Sky Blues from Bradford City in the summer of 2019 and has since firmly established himself as Coventry City's first choice goalkeeper.

The 31-year-old stopper was in excellent form during 2022/23, helping the Sky Blues reach the Championship Play-Off final. Wilson ended last season with the EFL Golden Glove award as the Championship 'keeper with the most clean sheets having registered a superb 20 league shut-outs.

His form was rewarded with a new contract in January 2023 as Wilson committed his future to the Sky Blue cause through until the end of the 2024/25 season.

ANSWERS

PAGE 29: FOOTY PHRASES

Keepie Uppie.

PAGE 34: A-Z QUIZ

A. Austrian. B. Burnley. C. Crystal Palace. D. Derby County. E. Egyptian. F. France. G. Goodison Park (Everton). H. Huddersfield Town. I. Iran. J. Jamaica. K. Kenilworth Road. L. Ladapo, Freddie. M. Middlesbrough (Chuba Akpom). N. Norwegian. O. Oldham Athletic. P. Pukki, Teemu. Q. Qatar. R. Real Madrid. S. Southampton. T. Toffolo, Harry. U. Undav, Deniz. V. Vardy, Jamie. W. Wilson, Ben (Coventry City). X. Xavier, Abel. Y. Yeovil Town. Z. Zenden, Boudewijn.

PAGE 42: FAN'TASTIC

PAGE 48: BEHIND THE BADGE

A. Tatsuhiro Sakamoto. B. Josh Eccles. C. Kyle McFadzean. D. Milan van Ewijk. E. Matt Godden. F. Kasey Palmer. G. Ellis Simms. H. Jake Bidwell.

PAGE 58: HIGH FIVES

QUIZ 1:

1. 2022/23, Viktor Gyökeres (21 goals).
2. 2021/23, Viktor Gyökeres (17 goals).
3. 2020/21, Tyler Walker (Seven goals).
4. 2019/20, Matt Godden (14 goals).
5. 2018/19, Jordy Hiwula (12 goals).

QUIZ 2:

1. 2022/23, Wrexham (third round.
2. 2021/22, Southampton (fourth round).
3. 2021/22, Derby County (third round).
4. 2020/21, Norwich City (third round).
5. 2019/20, Birmingham City (fourth round).

QUIZ 3:

1. Tony Mowbray. 2. Steven Pressley. 3. Mark Robins. 4. Andy Thorn.
5. Aidy Boothroyd.

QUIZ 4:

1. Bristol City (2022/23). 2. Northampton Town (2021/22).
3. Gillingham (2020/21). 4. Watford (2019/20). 5. Exeter City (2019/20).

QUIZ 5:

1. 5th in Championship (2022/23). 2. 12th in Championship (2021/22).
3. 16th in Championship (2020/21). 4. 1st in League One (2019/20)*.
5. 8th in League One (2018/19).

QUIZ 6:

1. Viktor Gyökeres (44 Championship starts).
2. Ben Wilson (43 Championship starts).
3. Jake Bidwell (40 Championship starts).
4. Gustavo Hamer and Callum Doyle (both had 39 Championship starts).
5. Jamie Allen and Kyle McFadzean (both had 34 Championship starts).

QUIZ 7:

1. 10. 2. 14. 3. 13. 4. 4. 5. 28.

QUIZ 8:

1. 2007/08, Coventry City 2-0 Leicester City (Championship).
2. 2000/01, Leicester City 1-3 Coventry City (Premier League).
3. 2000/01, Coventry City 1-0 Leicester City (Premier League).
4. 1988/99, Leicester City 0-3 Coventry City (FA Cup).
5. 1996/97, Leicester City 0-2 Coventry City (Premier League).

QUIZ 9:

1. Coventry City 2-0 Birmingham City. 2. Coventry City 2-1 Reading.
3. Queens Park Rangers 0-3 Coventry City. 4. Blackpool 1-4 Coventry City.
5. Huddersfield Town 0-4 Coventry City.

QUIZ 10:

1. 2022/23, 70 points. 2. 2021/22, 64 points. 3. 2020/21, 55 points.
4. 2019/20, 67 points**. 5. 2018/19, 65 points.

* Table decided on points-per-game basis.
** Points won before season curtailed.

CLASSIC FAN'TASTIC